50 Autumn October Season Dishes

By: Kelly Johnson

Table of Contents

- Pumpkin Soup
- Butternut Squash Risotto
- Apple Cider Glazed Chicken
- Roasted Sweet Potatoes
- Caramelized Onion Tart
- Pumpkin Pie
- Cinnamon Roasted Apples
- Chestnut Soup
- Beef Stew
- Maple Roasted Brussels Sprouts
- Spaghetti Squash Primavera
- Mushroom Risotto
- Baked Acorn Squash
- Cranberry Sauce
- Roast Pork with Apple Chutney
- Pumpkin Bread
- Apple Cinnamon Pancakes
- Roasted Root Vegetables
- Autumn Harvest Salad

- Pear and Gorgonzola Salad
- Stuffed Delicata Squash
- Sweet Potato Casserole
- Pecan Pie
- Cranberry Pecan Bread
- Maple-Glazed Carrots
- Spiced Pear Cake
- Roasted Cauliflower Soup
- Beef and Pumpkin Chili
- Autumn Vegetable Stew
- Spicy Butternut Squash Soup
- Pumpkin Risotto
- Apple and Cheddar Grilled Cheese
- Mushroom and Leek Pie
- Cider-Braised Chicken
- Maple-Glazed Brussels Sprouts
- Butternut Squash Mac and Cheese
- Spiced Pumpkin Muffins
- Savory Herb Stuffing
- Roast Turkey with Cranberry Sauce
- Potato Leek Soup

- Autumn Chili with Cornbread
- Roasted Pumpkin Seeds
- Cinnamon Baked Pears
- Apple Crisp
- Squash and Spinach Lasagna
- Carrot Ginger Soup
- Autumn Apple Slaw
- Harvest Grain Bowl
- Roasted Pumpkin Soup
- Wild Mushroom Soup

Pumpkin Soup

Ingredients:

- 1 medium pumpkin, peeled and cubed
- 1 onion, chopped
- 2 cloves garlic, minced
- 4 cups vegetable broth
- 1/2 cup coconut milk or cream
- 1 tsp ground cinnamon
- 1/2 tsp ground nutmeg
- Salt and pepper to taste
- 2 tbsp olive oil

Instructions:

1. Heat olive oil in a large pot over medium heat. Add onion and garlic, sautéing until softened.
2. Add cubed pumpkin, vegetable broth, cinnamon, and nutmeg. Bring to a boil, then simmer for 20-25 minutes until pumpkin is tender.
3. Use an immersion blender to puree the soup until smooth, or transfer to a blender in batches.
4. Stir in coconut milk or cream and season with salt and pepper. Serve warm.

Butternut Squash Risotto

Ingredients:

- 1 small butternut squash, peeled and cubed
- 1 1/2 cups Arborio rice
- 4 cups vegetable broth
- 1/2 cup dry white wine (optional)
- 1/2 onion, chopped
- 2 cloves garlic, minced
- 1/2 cup grated Parmesan cheese
- 2 tbsp butter
- 2 tbsp olive oil
- Salt and pepper to taste

Instructions:

1. In a large pan, heat olive oil over medium heat. Add chopped onion and garlic, sautéing until translucent.

2. Add the butternut squash cubes and cook for 5 minutes. Pour in the white wine (if using) and cook for 1-2 minutes.

3. Stir in Arborio rice and cook for 1 minute, then begin adding broth, one cup at a time, stirring occasionally until the liquid is absorbed before adding more.

4. Continue cooking for about 20 minutes, until rice is tender and creamy. Stir in butter and Parmesan cheese, and season with salt and pepper.

Apple Cider Glazed Chicken

Ingredients:

- 4 boneless, skinless chicken breasts
- 1 cup apple cider
- 1 tbsp olive oil
- 1/2 onion, chopped
- 2 cloves garlic, minced
- 1 tbsp Dijon mustard
- 1 tbsp apple cider vinegar
- 1 tbsp fresh thyme (or 1 tsp dried thyme)
- Salt and pepper to taste

Instructions:

1. Heat olive oil in a skillet over medium heat. Season chicken breasts with salt and pepper and cook until browned on both sides, about 5-6 minutes per side. Remove chicken and set aside.

2. In the same skillet, sauté onion and garlic until soft, about 3 minutes.

3. Add apple cider, Dijon mustard, apple cider vinegar, and thyme. Bring to a simmer and cook for 5-7 minutes, until the sauce thickens slightly.

4. Return chicken to the skillet and simmer for 10 minutes, spooning sauce over the chicken as it cooks. Serve with the apple cider glaze.

Roasted Sweet Potatoes

Ingredients:

- 4 medium sweet potatoes, peeled and cubed
- 2 tbsp olive oil
- 1 tsp ground cinnamon
- 1/2 tsp ground paprika
- Salt and pepper to taste
- 1 tbsp fresh parsley, chopped (optional)

Instructions:

1. Preheat oven to 400°F (200°C). Toss sweet potato cubes with olive oil, cinnamon, paprika, salt, and pepper.
2. Spread potatoes in a single layer on a baking sheet and roast for 25-30 minutes, turning halfway through, until tender and golden brown.
3. Garnish with fresh parsley before serving.

Caramelized Onion Tart

Ingredients:

- 1 sheet puff pastry
- 2 large onions, thinly sliced
- 2 tbsp olive oil
- 1 tbsp balsamic vinegar
- 1 tsp fresh thyme (or 1/3 tsp dried thyme)
- 1/2 cup grated Gruyère cheese
- Salt and pepper to taste

Instructions:

1. Preheat oven to 400°F (200°C). Heat olive oil in a skillet over medium heat. Add onions and cook for 20-25 minutes, stirring occasionally, until onions are soft and golden.
2. Add balsamic vinegar and thyme to the onions and cook for another 2-3 minutes. Season with salt and pepper.
3. Roll out puff pastry on a baking sheet. Spread the caramelized onions evenly over the pastry.
4. Sprinkle with grated Gruyère cheese and bake for 20-25 minutes, until the pastry is golden and puffed.

Pumpkin Pie

Ingredients:

- 1 1/2 cups canned pumpkin puree
- 3/4 cup brown sugar
- 2 eggs
- 1 cup heavy cream
- 1 tsp ground cinnamon
- 1/2 tsp ground ginger
- 1/4 tsp ground nutmeg
- 1/4 tsp ground cloves
- 1/2 tsp vanilla extract
- 1 pie crust (store-bought or homemade)

Instructions:

1. Preheat oven to 375°F (190°C). In a large bowl, whisk together pumpkin puree, brown sugar, eggs, heavy cream, spices, and vanilla extract.
2. Pour the pumpkin mixture into the pie crust and smooth the top.
3. Bake for 45-50 minutes, until the center is set and a toothpick inserted into the center comes out clean.
4. Let the pie cool completely before serving.

Cinnamon Roasted Apples

Ingredients:

- 4 large apples, peeled, cored, and sliced
- 2 tbsp butter, melted
- 1/4 cup brown sugar
- 1 tsp ground cinnamon
- 1/4 tsp ground nutmeg
- Pinch of salt

Instructions:

1. Preheat oven to 375°F (190°C). In a bowl, toss apple slices with melted butter, brown sugar, cinnamon, nutmeg, and salt.
2. Spread apples on a baking sheet in a single layer.
3. Roast for 25-30 minutes, stirring once, until apples are tender and caramelized.

Chestnut Soup

Ingredients:

- 2 cups roasted chestnuts, peeled and chopped
- 1 onion, chopped
- 2 cloves garlic, minced
- 4 cups vegetable or chicken broth
- 1/2 cup heavy cream
- 2 tbsp olive oil
- 1 tsp fresh thyme (or 1/3 tsp dried thyme)
- Salt and pepper to taste

Instructions:

1. Heat olive oil in a large pot over medium heat. Add onion and garlic, sautéing until soft.
2. Add chestnuts and cook for 2-3 minutes. Pour in broth and thyme, then bring to a boil.
3. Simmer for 20 minutes, then use an immersion blender to puree the soup until smooth.
4. Stir in heavy cream, season with salt and pepper, and serve warm.

Beef Stew

Ingredients:

- 1 lb beef stew meat, cubed
- 4 cups beef broth
- 4 medium potatoes, cubed
- 3 carrots, sliced
- 2 celery stalks, chopped
- 1 onion, chopped
- 2 cloves garlic, minced
- 1 tsp dried thyme
- 2 tbsp flour
- 2 tbsp olive oil
- Salt and pepper to taste

Instructions:

1. Heat olive oil in a large pot over medium heat. Brown beef stew meat in batches, removing each batch to set aside.
2. In the same pot, sauté onion and garlic until soft. Sprinkle flour over the onions and stir for 1 minute.
3. Return beef to the pot along with broth, thyme, potatoes, carrots, and celery. Bring to a boil.
4. Reduce heat and simmer for 1-1.5 hours, until the beef is tender and the stew thickens. Season with salt and pepper.

Maple Roasted Brussels Sprouts

Ingredients:

- 1 lb Brussels sprouts, trimmed and halved
- 2 tbsp olive oil
- 2 tbsp maple syrup
- 1 tbsp balsamic vinegar
- Salt and pepper to taste

Instructions:

1. Preheat oven to 400°F (200°C). Toss Brussels sprouts with olive oil, maple syrup, balsamic vinegar, salt, and pepper.
2. Spread Brussels sprouts in a single layer on a baking sheet.
3. Roast for 20-25 minutes, flipping halfway through, until crispy and caramelized.
4. Serve warm.

Spaghetti Squash Primavera

Ingredients:

- 1 medium spaghetti squash
- 1 tbsp olive oil
- 1 bell pepper, chopped
- 1 zucchini, sliced
- 1 cup cherry tomatoes, halved
- 1/2 onion, chopped
- 2 cloves garlic, minced
- 1/2 cup grated Parmesan cheese
- Fresh basil, chopped (optional)
- Salt and pepper to taste

Instructions:

1. Preheat oven to 400°F (200°C). Slice spaghetti squash in half and remove seeds. Drizzle with olive oil, salt, and pepper.
2. Place squash halves cut-side down on a baking sheet and roast for 40-45 minutes, until tender.
3. Meanwhile, heat olive oil in a pan over medium heat. Sauté bell pepper, zucchini, onion, and garlic for 5-7 minutes.
4. Use a fork to scrape the flesh of the roasted squash into spaghetti-like strands.
5. Toss the squash with the sautéed vegetables, cherry tomatoes, Parmesan cheese, and fresh basil. Serve warm.

Mushroom Risotto

Ingredients:

- 1 1/2 cups Arborio rice
- 2 cups mushrooms, sliced (button or cremini)
- 4 cups vegetable broth
- 1/2 cup dry white wine (optional)
- 1/2 onion, chopped
- 2 cloves garlic, minced
- 1/2 cup grated Parmesan cheese
- 2 tbsp butter
- 2 tbsp olive oil
- Salt and pepper to taste

Instructions:

1. Heat olive oil and butter in a pan over medium heat. Add onions and garlic, sautéing until soft.
2. Add mushrooms and cook for 5-7 minutes until browned.
3. Stir in Arborio rice and cook for 1 minute.
4. Gradually add broth, one cup at a time, stirring frequently, and allowing liquid to absorb before adding more. Continue until rice is creamy and tender (about 20 minutes).
5. Stir in Parmesan cheese and season with salt and pepper. Serve warm.

Baked Acorn Squash

Ingredients:

- 2 acorn squashes, halved and seeded
- 2 tbsp olive oil
- 1 tbsp maple syrup
- Salt and pepper to taste
- 1/4 cup pecans, chopped (optional)

Instructions:

1. Preheat oven to 375°F (190°C). Place squash halves cut-side up on a baking sheet.
2. Drizzle with olive oil and maple syrup, then season with salt and pepper.
3. Roast for 30-35 minutes, until tender and caramelized.
4. Sprinkle with chopped pecans before serving.

Cranberry Sauce

Ingredients:

- 12 oz fresh or frozen cranberries
- 1/2 cup sugar
- 1/2 cup orange juice
- 1 tsp orange zest
- 1/2 tsp ground cinnamon

Instructions:

1. In a saucepan, combine cranberries, sugar, orange juice, orange zest, and cinnamon.
2. Bring to a boil, then reduce to a simmer and cook for 10-15 minutes, until cranberries burst and sauce thickens.
3. Let cool before serving.

Roast Pork with Apple Chutney

Ingredients:

- 1 1/2 lb pork loin roast
- 2 tbsp olive oil
- 1 tsp dried rosemary
- Salt and pepper to taste
- 2 apples, peeled, cored, and chopped
- 1/4 cup onion, chopped
- 1/4 cup brown sugar
- 2 tbsp apple cider vinegar
- 1/2 tsp ground cinnamon
- 1/4 tsp ground ginger

Instructions:

1. Preheat oven to 375°F (190°C). Season pork roast with olive oil, rosemary, salt, and pepper.
2. Roast pork in the oven for 40-45 minutes, until the internal temperature reaches 145°F (63°C).
3. While the pork is roasting, combine apples, onion, brown sugar, apple cider vinegar, cinnamon, and ginger in a saucepan.
4. Simmer over low heat for 15-20 minutes, stirring occasionally, until apples are soft and chutney thickens.
5. Slice pork and serve with apple chutney.

Pumpkin Bread

Ingredients:

- 1 1/2 cups all-purpose flour
- 1 tsp baking soda
- 1/2 tsp salt
- 1/2 tsp ground cinnamon
- 1/2 tsp ground nutmeg
- 1/2 cup vegetable oil
- 1 cup pumpkin puree
- 3/4 cup sugar
- 2 eggs
- 1 tsp vanilla extract

Instructions:

1. Preheat oven to 350°F (175°C). Grease a loaf pan.
2. In a bowl, whisk together flour, baking soda, salt, cinnamon, and nutmeg.
3. In another bowl, mix oil, pumpkin puree, sugar, eggs, and vanilla.
4. Gradually stir the dry ingredients into the wet ingredients until combined.
5. Pour the batter into the loaf pan and bake for 60-65 minutes, or until a toothpick comes out clean.
6. Let cool before slicing and serving.

Apple Cinnamon Pancakes

Ingredients:

- 1 1/2 cups all-purpose flour
- 2 tbsp sugar
- 1 tsp baking powder
- 1/2 tsp ground cinnamon
- 1/4 tsp salt
- 1 cup milk
- 1 egg
- 1/4 cup melted butter
- 1 apple, peeled, cored, and chopped
- 1/4 tsp vanilla extract

Instructions:

1. In a large bowl, whisk together flour, sugar, baking powder, cinnamon, and salt.
2. In a separate bowl, whisk together milk, egg, melted butter, and vanilla.
3. Pour the wet ingredients into the dry ingredients and stir until just combined. Fold in chopped apples.
4. Heat a griddle or pan over medium heat and lightly grease. Pour 1/4 cup batter for each pancake and cook until bubbles form, then flip and cook until golden brown on both sides.
5. Serve warm with syrup.

Roasted Root Vegetables

Ingredients:

- 2 large carrots, peeled and sliced
- 2 parsnips, peeled and sliced
- 2 sweet potatoes, peeled and cubed
- 1 tbsp olive oil
- 1 tbsp fresh rosemary, chopped
- Salt and pepper to taste

Instructions:

1. Preheat oven to 400°F (200°C). Toss carrots, parsnips, and sweet potatoes with olive oil, rosemary, salt, and pepper.
2. Spread the vegetables in a single layer on a baking sheet.
3. Roast for 30-35 minutes, turning halfway through, until tender and golden brown.
4. Serve warm.

Autumn Harvest Salad

Ingredients:

- 4 cups mixed greens (arugula, spinach, and kale)
- 1 apple, thinly sliced
- 1/2 cup pomegranate seeds
- 1/2 cup candied pecans
- 1/4 cup crumbled goat cheese
- 2 tbsp olive oil
- 1 tbsp balsamic vinegar
- Salt and pepper to taste

Instructions:

1. In a large bowl, combine mixed greens, apple slices, pomegranate seeds, candied pecans, and goat cheese.
2. In a small bowl, whisk together olive oil, balsamic vinegar, salt, and pepper.
3. Drizzle dressing over the salad and toss gently to combine. Serve immediately.

Pear and Gorgonzola Salad

Ingredients:

- 4 cups mixed greens (arugula, spinach, and lettuce)
- 2 pears, sliced
- 1/2 cup crumbled Gorgonzola cheese
- 1/4 cup walnuts, toasted
- 2 tbsp olive oil
- 1 tbsp honey
- 1 tbsp red wine vinegar
- Salt and pepper to taste

Instructions:

1. In a large bowl, combine mixed greens, pear slices, Gorgonzola cheese, and toasted walnuts.
2. In a small bowl, whisk together olive oil, honey, red wine vinegar, salt, and pepper.
3. Drizzle the dressing over the salad and toss to combine. Serve immediately.

Stuffed Delicata Squash

Ingredients:

- 2 delicata squashes, halved and seeded
- 1 tbsp olive oil
- 1/2 cup quinoa, cooked
- 1/4 cup dried cranberries
- 1/4 cup pecans, chopped
- 1/4 cup feta cheese, crumbled
- 1 tbsp fresh thyme leaves
- Salt and pepper to taste

Instructions:

1. Preheat oven to 375°F (190°C). Drizzle the squash halves with olive oil and season with salt and pepper.
2. Place the squash halves cut-side down on a baking sheet and roast for 30-35 minutes, until tender.
3. In a bowl, mix cooked quinoa, dried cranberries, pecans, feta, and thyme.
4. Once the squash is done, stuff the halves with the quinoa mixture and return to the oven for 10 minutes to warm through.
5. Serve immediately.

Sweet Potato Casserole

Ingredients:

- 4 medium sweet potatoes, peeled and cubed
- 1/4 cup butter, melted
- 1/4 cup brown sugar
- 1/2 tsp cinnamon
- 1/4 tsp nutmeg
- 1/2 cup milk
- 1 tsp vanilla extract
- 1 cup mini marshmallows (optional)

Instructions:

1. Preheat oven to 350°F (175°C). Boil sweet potatoes in a large pot for 10-12 minutes, until tender.
2. Drain potatoes and mash them with melted butter, brown sugar, cinnamon, nutmeg, milk, and vanilla.
3. Transfer to a baking dish and top with mini marshmallows, if using.
4. Bake for 20-25 minutes, until the marshmallows are golden brown.
5. Serve warm.

Pecan Pie

Ingredients:

- 1 pie crust (store-bought or homemade)
- 1 1/2 cups pecans, chopped
- 3/4 cup corn syrup
- 1/2 cup brown sugar
- 3 large eggs
- 1/4 cup butter, melted
- 1 tsp vanilla extract
- 1/4 tsp salt

Instructions:

1. Preheat oven to 350°F (175°C). Line a pie pan with the pie crust.
2. In a large bowl, whisk together corn syrup, brown sugar, eggs, melted butter, vanilla extract, and salt.
3. Stir in chopped pecans and pour the mixture into the pie crust.
4. Bake for 45-50 minutes, until the center is set and the crust is golden.
5. Let cool before slicing and serving.

Cranberry Pecan Bread

Ingredients:

- 2 cups all-purpose flour
- 1 tsp baking soda
- 1/2 tsp salt
- 1 tsp ground cinnamon
- 1 cup sugar
- 1/2 cup unsalted butter, softened
- 2 large eggs
- 1 cup fresh or frozen cranberries, chopped
- 1/2 cup pecans, chopped
- 1/4 cup orange juice
- 1 tsp vanilla extract

Instructions:

1. Preheat oven to 350°F (175°C). Grease a loaf pan.
2. In a bowl, mix flour, baking soda, salt, and cinnamon.
3. In another bowl, cream butter and sugar together, then add eggs one at a time, beating well after each addition.
4. Stir in the flour mixture, cranberries, pecans, orange juice, and vanilla.
5. Pour the batter into the prepared pan and bake for 55-60 minutes, until a toothpick comes out clean.
6. Let cool before slicing and serving.

Maple-Glazed Carrots

Ingredients:

- 1 lb baby carrots
- 2 tbsp butter
- 1/4 cup maple syrup
- 1 tbsp fresh thyme, chopped
- Salt and pepper to taste

Instructions:

1. Boil carrots in a pot of water for 6-8 minutes, until tender.
2. Drain the carrots and set aside.
3. In a skillet, melt butter over medium heat and stir in maple syrup, thyme, salt, and pepper.
4. Add the cooked carrots and toss to coat. Cook for 2-3 minutes, until glazed.
5. Serve warm.

Spiced Pear Cake

Ingredients:

- 2 pears, peeled and diced
- 1 1/2 cups all-purpose flour
- 1 tsp baking powder
- 1/2 tsp ground cinnamon
- 1/4 tsp ground nutmeg
- 1/2 tsp salt
- 1/2 cup sugar
- 1/4 cup butter, softened
- 2 large eggs
- 1 tsp vanilla extract
- 1/2 cup milk

Instructions:

1. Preheat oven to 350°F (175°C). Grease and flour a baking pan.
2. In a bowl, whisk together flour, baking powder, cinnamon, nutmeg, and salt.
3. In another bowl, cream butter and sugar together, then add eggs one at a time. Stir in vanilla.
4. Gradually add the dry ingredients, alternating with milk, until just combined.
5. Gently fold in the diced pears.
6. Pour the batter into the prepared pan and bake for 35-40 minutes, until a toothpick comes out clean.

Roasted Cauliflower Soup

Ingredients:

- 1 head of cauliflower, cut into florets
- 1 tbsp olive oil
- 1 onion, chopped
- 2 cloves garlic, minced
- 4 cups vegetable broth
- 1/2 cup heavy cream
- 1/2 tsp ground cumin
- Salt and pepper to taste

Instructions:

1. Preheat oven to 400°F (200°C). Toss cauliflower florets with olive oil, salt, and pepper, and spread on a baking sheet.
2. Roast for 20-25 minutes, until golden and tender.
3. In a large pot, sauté onion and garlic until soft. Add cumin and cook for another minute.
4. Add roasted cauliflower and vegetable broth, bringing to a boil.
5. Simmer for 10 minutes, then use an immersion blender to puree the soup until smooth.
6. Stir in heavy cream and season with salt and pepper. Serve warm.

Beef and Pumpkin Chili

Ingredients:

- 1 lb ground beef
- 1 onion, chopped
- 2 cloves garlic, minced
- 1 can (15 oz) pumpkin puree
- 1 can (15 oz) diced tomatoes
- 1 can (15 oz) kidney beans, drained and rinsed
- 1 tbsp chili powder
- 1 tsp ground cumin
- 1/2 tsp smoked paprika
- 2 cups beef broth
- Salt and pepper to taste

Instructions:

1. In a large pot, cook ground beef over medium heat until browned. Add onion and garlic and cook until softened.
2. Stir in pumpkin puree, diced tomatoes, kidney beans, chili powder, cumin, smoked paprika, and beef broth.
3. Bring to a simmer and cook for 30 minutes. Season with salt and pepper.
4. Serve warm, garnished with sour cream or cheese if desired.

Autumn Vegetable Stew

Ingredients:

- 2 tbsp olive oil
- 1 onion, chopped
- 3 carrots, peeled and sliced
- 2 parsnips, peeled and sliced
- 1 small butternut squash, peeled and cubed
- 2 cups vegetable broth
- 1 can (15 oz) diced tomatoes
- 1 tsp dried thyme
- 1/2 tsp ground cinnamon
- Salt and pepper to taste
- Fresh parsley for garnish

Instructions:

1. Heat olive oil in a large pot over medium heat. Add onion and cook until softened.
2. Add carrots, parsnips, butternut squash, vegetable broth, diced tomatoes, thyme, cinnamon, salt, and pepper.
3. Bring to a boil, then reduce to a simmer and cook for 30 minutes, until vegetables are tender.
4. Serve hot, garnished with fresh parsley.

Spicy Butternut Squash Soup

Ingredients:

- 1 tbsp olive oil
- 1 onion, chopped
- 2 cloves garlic, minced
- 1 butternut squash, peeled, seeded, and cubed
- 4 cups vegetable broth
- 1 tsp ground cumin
- 1/2 tsp ground cinnamon
- 1/4 tsp ground cayenne pepper (adjust to taste)
- Salt and pepper to taste
- 1/2 cup coconut milk (optional)

Instructions:

1. Heat olive oil in a pot over medium heat. Add onion and garlic and cook until softened.
2. Stir in butternut squash, vegetable broth, cumin, cinnamon, cayenne, salt, and pepper.
3. Bring to a boil, then reduce heat and simmer for 25-30 minutes, until squash is tender.
4. Use an immersion blender to puree the soup until smooth.
5. Stir in coconut milk if desired and adjust seasoning before serving.

Pumpkin Risotto

Ingredients:

- 2 tbsp butter
- 1 onion, chopped
- 2 cloves garlic, minced
- 1 1/2 cups Arborio rice
- 1 can (15 oz) pumpkin puree
- 4 cups vegetable broth, warm
- 1/2 cup dry white wine
- 1/2 cup Parmesan cheese, grated
- Salt and pepper to taste
- Fresh sage for garnish

Instructions:

1. In a large pan, melt butter over medium heat. Add onion and garlic and cook until softened.
2. Stir in Arborio rice and cook for 1-2 minutes, until the rice is lightly toasted.
3. Pour in white wine and stir until absorbed. Gradually add warm vegetable broth, one ladle at a time, stirring frequently, until the liquid is absorbed before adding more.
4. When the rice is tender and creamy, stir in pumpkin puree and Parmesan cheese. Season with salt and pepper.
5. Serve warm, garnished with fresh sage.

Apple and Cheddar Grilled Cheese

Ingredients:

- 2 slices whole wheat bread
- 2 tbsp butter
- 1/4 cup cheddar cheese, grated
- 1/4 apple, thinly sliced
- 1 tsp honey (optional)

Instructions:

1. Butter one side of each slice of bread.
2. On the unbuttered side of one slice, layer cheddar cheese and apple slices. Drizzle with honey if desired.
3. Place the other slice of bread on top, buttered side out.
4. Cook in a skillet over medium heat for 3-4 minutes on each side, until golden brown and the cheese is melted.
5. Serve warm.

Mushroom and Leek Pie

Ingredients:

- 1 tbsp olive oil
- 1 onion, chopped
- 2 leeks, cleaned and sliced
- 2 cups mushrooms, sliced
- 1/2 cup vegetable broth
- 1/2 cup heavy cream
- 1 tsp dried thyme
- Salt and pepper to taste
- 1 sheet puff pastry, thawed

Instructions:

1. Preheat oven to 375°F (190°C).
2. In a skillet, heat olive oil over medium heat. Add onion, leeks, and mushrooms and cook until softened.
3. Stir in vegetable broth, heavy cream, thyme, salt, and pepper. Simmer for 5 minutes, until the mixture thickens.
4. Roll out puff pastry on a baking sheet and spoon the mushroom mixture onto the center.
5. Fold the edges of the pastry over the filling, leaving the center exposed.
6. Bake for 25-30 minutes, until the pastry is golden brown and puffed.

Cider-Braised Chicken

Ingredients:

- 4 chicken thighs, bone-in and skin-on
- 1 tbsp olive oil
- 1 onion, chopped
- 2 cloves garlic, minced
- 1 cup apple cider
- 1/2 cup chicken broth
- 2 sprigs fresh thyme
- Salt and pepper to taste

Instructions:

1. Heat olive oil in a skillet over medium-high heat. Season chicken thighs with salt and pepper, and sear on both sides until golden brown.
2. Remove chicken and set aside. Add onion and garlic to the skillet and cook until softened.
3. Pour in apple cider and chicken broth, scraping up any brown bits from the skillet.
4. Return chicken to the skillet and add thyme. Cover and simmer for 35-40 minutes, until chicken is cooked through and tender.
5. Serve the chicken with the braising sauce.

Maple-Glazed Brussels Sprouts

Ingredients:

- 1 lb Brussels sprouts, trimmed and halved
- 2 tbsp olive oil
- 2 tbsp maple syrup
- 1 tbsp balsamic vinegar
- Salt and pepper to taste

Instructions:

1. Preheat oven to 400°F (200°C). Toss Brussels sprouts with olive oil, salt, and pepper.
2. Spread Brussels sprouts on a baking sheet in a single layer and roast for 20-25 minutes, flipping halfway through.
3. In a small bowl, whisk together maple syrup and balsamic vinegar. Drizzle over the roasted Brussels sprouts and toss to coat.
4. Serve warm.

Butternut Squash Mac and Cheese

Ingredients:

- 1 lb elbow macaroni
- 2 tbsp butter
- 1 small butternut squash, peeled, cubed, and roasted
- 2 cups milk
- 1 cup shredded cheddar cheese
- 1/2 cup grated Parmesan cheese
- 1/4 tsp ground nutmeg
- Salt and pepper to taste

Instructions:

1. Cook macaroni according to package instructions and set aside.
2. In a blender, puree the roasted butternut squash with milk until smooth.
3. In a pot, melt butter over medium heat. Stir in squash puree, cheddar cheese, Parmesan cheese, nutmeg, salt, and pepper.
4. Add cooked macaroni to the cheese sauce and toss to coat.
5. Serve warm.

Spiced Pumpkin Muffins

Ingredients:

- 1 3/4 cups all-purpose flour
- 1 tsp baking soda
- 1/2 tsp baking powder
- 1/2 tsp salt
- 1 tsp ground cinnamon
- 1/2 tsp ground nutmeg
- 1/4 tsp ground cloves
- 1/2 cup vegetable oil
- 1 cup canned pumpkin puree
- 1 cup sugar
- 2 large eggs
- 1 tsp vanilla extract
- 1/2 cup chopped walnuts or pecans (optional)

Instructions:

1. Preheat oven to 350°F (175°C) and line a muffin tin with paper liners.
2. In a bowl, whisk together flour, baking soda, baking powder, salt, cinnamon, nutmeg, and cloves.
3. In another bowl, whisk together oil, pumpkin, sugar, eggs, and vanilla.
4. Gradually stir in the dry ingredients until just combined. Fold in nuts if desired.
5. Spoon batter into muffin cups, filling each about 2/3 full.

6. Bake for 20-25 minutes, or until a toothpick inserted comes out clean. Cool before serving.

Savory Herb Stuffing

Ingredients:

- 1 loaf bread, cubed and dried
- 2 tbsp butter
- 1 onion, chopped
- 2 celery stalks, chopped
- 2 cloves garlic, minced
- 1/2 tsp dried sage
- 1/2 tsp dried thyme
- 1/2 tsp ground black pepper
- 2 cups vegetable broth
- 1/2 cup fresh parsley, chopped
- Salt to taste

Instructions:

1. Preheat oven to 350°F (175°C) and grease a baking dish.
2. In a pan, melt butter over medium heat. Add onion, celery, and garlic, and cook until softened.
3. Stir in sage, thyme, pepper, and a pinch of salt. Remove from heat.
4. In a large bowl, combine the dried bread cubes with the vegetable broth and parsley. Add the sautéed vegetables and mix well.
5. Transfer the mixture to the baking dish and cover with foil. Bake for 30 minutes.
6. Remove foil and bake for an additional 10 minutes, until golden brown.

Roast Turkey with Cranberry Sauce

Ingredients:

- 1 whole turkey (10-12 lbs)
- 4 tbsp olive oil
- 1 tbsp salt
- 1 tbsp pepper
- 1 onion, quartered
- 2 sprigs rosemary
- 1 lemon, halved
- 1 cup chicken broth
- 2 cups fresh cranberries
- 1/2 cup sugar
- 1/2 cup water

Instructions:

1. Preheat oven to 375°F (190°C). Rub turkey with olive oil, salt, and pepper. Stuff the turkey with onion, rosemary, and lemon.

2. Place turkey in a roasting pan and pour chicken broth around it. Roast for 3-4 hours, basting every 30 minutes, until the internal temperature reaches 165°F (74°C).

3. For cranberry sauce, combine cranberries, sugar, and water in a saucepan over medium heat. Cook for 10-15 minutes, until the berries burst and the sauce thickens.

4. Serve turkey with fresh cranberry sauce on the side.

Potato Leek Soup

Ingredients:

- 2 tbsp butter
- 3 leeks, cleaned and sliced
- 4 medium potatoes, peeled and cubed
- 4 cups vegetable broth
- 1 cup heavy cream
- Salt and pepper to taste
- Fresh chives, chopped (for garnish)

Instructions:

1. In a pot, melt butter over medium heat. Add leeks and cook until softened.
2. Add potatoes and vegetable broth, bringing to a boil. Reduce heat and simmer for 20-25 minutes, until potatoes are tender.
3. Use an immersion blender to puree the soup until smooth, or leave it chunky if preferred.
4. Stir in heavy cream, and season with salt and pepper.
5. Serve garnished with chopped chives.

Autumn Chili with Cornbread

Ingredients:

- 1 lb ground beef or turkey
- 1 onion, chopped
- 2 cloves garlic, minced
- 1 can (15 oz) pumpkin puree
- 1 can (15 oz) diced tomatoes
- 2 cups kidney beans, drained and rinsed
- 1 tbsp chili powder
- 1 tsp cumin
- 1/2 tsp smoked paprika
- 2 cups vegetable broth
- Salt and pepper to taste

Cornbread:

- 1 cup cornmeal
- 1 cup all-purpose flour
- 1 tbsp baking powder
- 1/4 cup sugar
- 1/2 tsp salt
- 1 cup milk
- 2 eggs
- 1/4 cup melted butter

Instructions:

1. For chili, cook ground beef or turkey with onion and garlic until browned. Stir in pumpkin, tomatoes, beans, chili powder, cumin, paprika, and vegetable broth.

2. Bring to a simmer and cook for 30 minutes. Season with salt and pepper to taste.

3. For cornbread, preheat oven to 375°F (190°C). Mix dry ingredients in one bowl and wet ingredients in another.

4. Combine the wet and dry ingredients, then pour into a greased baking dish. Bake for 25-30 minutes.

5. Serve chili with cornbread.

Roasted Pumpkin Seeds

Ingredients:

- 1 pumpkin, seeds removed
- 2 tbsp olive oil
- 1 tsp salt
- 1/2 tsp smoked paprika
- 1/2 tsp ground cinnamon

Instructions:

1. Preheat oven to 350°F (175°C).
2. Clean pumpkin seeds and spread them on a baking sheet.
3. Drizzle with olive oil and sprinkle with salt, paprika, and cinnamon.
4. Roast for 20-25 minutes, stirring occasionally, until golden brown and crispy.

Cinnamon Baked Pears

Ingredients:

- 4 ripe pears, halved and cored
- 1/4 cup honey
- 1 tsp ground cinnamon
- 1/4 tsp ground nutmeg
- 1 tbsp butter

Instructions:

1. Preheat oven to 350°F (175°C). Place pear halves in a baking dish.
2. Drizzle with honey and sprinkle with cinnamon and nutmeg. Place a small pat of butter on top of each pear half.
3. Bake for 25-30 minutes, until pears are tender. Serve warm.

Apple Crisp

Ingredients:

- 6 apples, peeled and sliced
- 1/2 cup sugar
- 1/2 tsp ground cinnamon
- 1 tbsp lemon juice
- 1/2 cup rolled oats
- 1/4 cup all-purpose flour
- 1/4 cup brown sugar
- 1/4 cup butter, melted

Instructions:

1. Preheat oven to 350°F (175°C). Arrange apple slices in a greased baking dish.
2. In a bowl, mix sugar, cinnamon, and lemon juice, and sprinkle over apples.
3. In another bowl, combine oats, flour, brown sugar, and melted butter. Sprinkle over apples.
4. Bake for 30-40 minutes, until golden brown and bubbly.

Squash and Spinach Lasagna

Ingredients:

- 1 small butternut squash, peeled and sliced thinly
- 2 cups fresh spinach, chopped
- 9 lasagna noodles, cooked
- 1 jar marinara sauce
- 1 cup ricotta cheese
- 1 1/2 cups shredded mozzarella cheese
- 1/2 cup grated Parmesan cheese
- 1 egg, beaten
- Salt and pepper to taste

Instructions:

1. Preheat oven to 375°F (190°C). In a bowl, combine ricotta cheese, egg, spinach, salt, and pepper.

2. In a baking dish, spread a thin layer of marinara sauce. Layer lasagna noodles, ricotta mixture, squash slices, and mozzarella cheese. Repeat layers, ending with a layer of marinara sauce and Parmesan cheese.

3. Cover with foil and bake for 30 minutes. Remove foil and bake for another 10 minutes until bubbly and golden brown. Serve warm.

Carrot Ginger Soup

Ingredients:

- 1 tbsp olive oil
- 1 onion, chopped
- 3 cups carrots, peeled and chopped
- 2 tsp fresh ginger, grated
- 4 cups vegetable broth
- 1/2 cup coconut milk
- Salt and pepper to taste
- Fresh parsley for garnish

Instructions:

1. Heat olive oil in a pot over medium heat. Add onion and cook until softened.
2. Add carrots and ginger, stirring for 1-2 minutes.
3. Pour in vegetable broth, bring to a boil, and then reduce to a simmer. Cook for 25-30 minutes, until carrots are tender.
4. Use an immersion blender to puree the soup until smooth.
5. Stir in coconut milk and season with salt and pepper. Serve garnished with fresh parsley.

Autumn Apple Slaw

Ingredients:

- 2 cups shredded cabbage
- 1 large apple, julienned
- 1/2 cup shredded carrots
- 1/4 cup chopped walnuts
- 1/4 cup dried cranberries
- 2 tbsp apple cider vinegar
- 1 tbsp honey
- 2 tbsp olive oil
- Salt and pepper to taste

Instructions:

1. In a large bowl, combine cabbage, apple, carrots, walnuts, and cranberries.
2. In a small bowl, whisk together apple cider vinegar, honey, olive oil, salt, and pepper.
3. Pour dressing over slaw and toss to combine.
4. Let sit for 10 minutes to allow flavors to meld before serving.

Harvest Grain Bowl

Ingredients:

- 1 cup quinoa or farro, cooked
- 1 small sweet potato, roasted and cubed
- 1/2 cup roasted Brussels sprouts
- 1/2 cup chickpeas, roasted
- 1/4 cup pomegranate seeds
- 2 tbsp tahini
- 1 tbsp lemon juice
- Salt and pepper to taste

Instructions:

1. In a large bowl, layer quinoa or farro, roasted sweet potato, Brussels sprouts, chickpeas, and pomegranate seeds.
2. In a small bowl, whisk together tahini, lemon juice, salt, and pepper.
3. Drizzle dressing over the bowl and toss to combine. Serve warm or at room temperature.

Roasted Pumpkin Soup

Ingredients:

- 1 small pumpkin, peeled, seeded, and cubed
- 1 tbsp olive oil
- 1 onion, chopped
- 2 cloves garlic, minced
- 4 cups vegetable broth
- 1 tsp ground cinnamon
- 1/2 tsp ground nutmeg
- Salt and pepper to taste
- 1/2 cup cream (optional)

Instructions:

1. Preheat oven to 400°F (200°C). Toss pumpkin cubes with olive oil and roast for 25-30 minutes until tender.
2. In a pot, sauté onion and garlic in olive oil until softened.
3. Add roasted pumpkin, vegetable broth, cinnamon, nutmeg, salt, and pepper. Bring to a simmer and cook for 10 minutes.
4. Use an immersion blender to puree the soup until smooth.
5. Stir in cream if desired and adjust seasoning before serving.

Wild Mushroom Soup

Ingredients:

- 2 tbsp butter
- 1 onion, chopped
- 2 cloves garlic, minced
- 3 cups mixed wild mushrooms, sliced
- 4 cups vegetable broth
- 1/2 cup heavy cream
- 1/4 cup fresh parsley, chopped
- Salt and pepper to taste

Instructions:

1. In a pot, melt butter over medium heat. Add onion and garlic, cooking until softened.
2. Add mushrooms and cook until they release their moisture and become tender.
3. Pour in vegetable broth and bring to a boil. Reduce to a simmer and cook for 15 minutes.
4. Use an immersion blender to blend the soup slightly for texture, or puree until smooth.
5. Stir in cream and fresh parsley. Season with salt and pepper before serving.

www.ingramcontent.com/pod-product-compliance
Lightning Source LLC
LaVergne TN
LVHW081321060526
838201LV00055B/2394